U0065802

智慧法語
止觀篇

心之道

Tranquility (śamatha)
and insight (vipassanā)

Illuminating one's mind
and recognizing one's
self-nature, cultivating
seamless wisdom

明心見性・生無漏智慧

第三輯

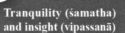

心道法師 語錄

By Dharma
Master Hsin Tao

目錄

Contents

**Tranquility (śamatha)
and insight (vipassanā) :**
Illuminating one's mind and
recognizing one's self-nature,
cultivating seamless wisdom

作者簡介

　　心道法師一九四八
年生，祖籍雲南，幼失
依怙，為滇緬邊境孤
雛。十三歲隨孤軍撤
移來台，十五歲初聞觀
音菩薩聖號，有感於觀
音菩薩的悲願，以「悟
性報觀音」、「吾不成
佛誓不休」、「真如度
眾生」刺身供佛，立誓

Tranquility (śamatha) and insight (vipassanā)
Illuminating one's mind and recognizing
one's self-nature, cultivating seamless wisdom

徹悟真理，救度苦難。

　　二十五歲出家後，
頭陀行腳歷十餘年，前
後在台北外雙溪、宜
蘭礁溪圓明寺、莿仔崙
墳塔、龍潭公墓和員
山周舉人廢墟，體驗
世間最幽隱不堪的「塚
間修」，矢志修證，了
脫生死，覺悟本來。

生道場」，展開弘法度
生的佛行事業，為現代
人擘劃成佛地圖。為了
推動宗教共存共榮，法
師以慈悲的華嚴理念奔
走國際，並於二〇〇一
年十一月成立世界宗教
博物館，致力於各種不
同宗教的對話，提昇對
所有宗教的寬容、尊重

著重基礎佛法戒、定、
慧的學習與薰陶，建立
佛法生活規範；「般若
期」著重在明瞭與貫徹
空性智慧；「法華期」
著重生起願力，發菩提
心；「華嚴期」則強調
多元共存、和諧共生，
證入圓滿無礙的境界。

　　心道法師以禪的

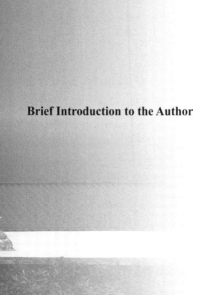

Brief Introduction to the Author

Born in upper Myanmar in 1948 to ethnic Chinese parents of Yunnan Province, Master Hsin Tao was left orphaned and impoverished at an early age. Having

been taken in by
the remnants of
ROC military units
operating along the
border of Yunnan,
China, he was brought
to Taiwan in 1961
when he was 13. At
the age of 15, he was

the Buddha, he had
himself tattooed
with the vows
"May I awaken
in gratitude for
the kindness of
Guanyin," "I will
never rest until
Buddhahood is

Tranquility (samatha) and insight (vipassanā)
Illuminating one's mind and recognizing
one's self-nature, cultivating seamless wisdom

enlightenment, Master Hsin Tao traveled on foot for over ten years, practicing austerities in lonely and secluded locations, including Waishuangxi in Taipei, Yuanming

the Fahua Cave on
Fulong Mountain in
early 1983, Master
Hsin Tao undertook
a fast which was to
last over two years,
during which time
he attained deep
insight into the

Tranquility (śamatha) and insight (vipassanā)
Illuminating one's mind and recognizing
one's self-nature, cultivating seamless wisdom

Master Hsin Tao felt great compassion for the suffering of all sentient beings. After his solitary retreat he established the Wusheng Monastery on the mountain in order to propagate

Tranquility (śamatha) and insight (vipassanā)
Illuminating one's mind and recognizing
one's self-nature, cultivating seamless wisdom

strived hard to
gain international
support with the
compassionate spirit
of the Buddhist
Avatamsaka Vision (of
the interconnectedness
of all beings in
the universe), and

is dedicated to
advancing the cause
of world peace
and a promoting
awareness of our
global family for
love and peace
through interreligious
dialogues. The

stage training
program," a
systematic and
comprehensive
approach applicable
to both monastics
and lay practitioners
alike to help
them deepen their

practice. First comes the āgama stage, which centers on the foundational teachings of Buddhism and the three-fold practice of morality, concentration, and wisdom. The prajñā

stage emphasizes the
theory and practice
of emptiness. The
dharmapuṇḍarīka
stage focuses on the
bodhisattva practice
of developing the
mind of enlightenment
through the power

Master Hsin Tao
has devoted himself
to propagating the
Dharma through
education, based on
the Chan principle
of quieting the mind
and seeing one's
original Buddha-

Tranquility (śamatha) and insight (vipassanā)
Illuminating one's mind and recognizing
one's self-nature, cultivating seamless wisdom

commitment, he leads people to devote themselves to the great cause of benefiting all sentient beings, ceaselessly helping them achieve liberating truth through

心之道第三輯 智慧法語

止觀篇－明心見性，生無漏智慧

The Way of Mind III:
Words of wisdom

**Tranquility (śamatha)
and insight (vipassanā):**
Illuminating one's mind and
recognizing one's self-nature,
cultivating seamless wisdom

「止」就是
攝心在一個地方；
「觀」就是
觀照一切如幻。

Tranquility (śamatha) and insight (vipassanā)
Illuminating one's mind and recognizing
one's self-nature, cultivating seamless wisdom

"Stopping" (śamatha)
means reining in the
mind and keeping it on a
certain object;
"observing" (vipassanā)
means seeing into the
illusory nature of all
phenomena.

如果我們能明悟本心，
就具有成佛的條件。

If you can understand
the original mind,
then you have the potential
for enlightenment.

Tranquility (śamatha) and insight (vipassanā)
Illuminating one's mind and recognizing
one's self-nature, cultivating seamless wisdom

Taking refuge
in the Triple Gem
amounts to setting out
on the path which leads to
enlightenment,
your essential nature,
and eternal life.

空行可以在「沒有」
顯現「有」，
住在「空」裡的靈性
就會經常顯現。

In the practice of emptiness,
"being" manifests in
"non-being";
the innate wisdom
which dwells in
emptiness shines forth.

心就是心，
不要隨著外境、好壞、
得失、美醜而轉。

The mind is just the mind;
don't let it be swayed
by changing external
conditions—good and bad,
gain and loss,
beauty and ugliness.

Tranquility (samatha) and insight (vipassanā)
Illuminating one's mind and recognizing
one's self-nature, cultivating seamless wisdom

Enlightenment is nothing
other than emptiness;
emptiness is none other
than Amitābha Buddha.

Tranquility (śamatha) and insight (vipassanā)
Illuminating one's mind and recognizing
one's self-nature, cultivating seamless wisdom

止觀篇
智慧法語

All conditions arise
from emptiness;
this is the eternal nature of
the Dharma-realm.

Tranquility (śamatha) and insight (vipassanā)
Illuminating one's mind and recognizing
one's self-nature, cultivating seamless wisdom

Bring the mind
to rest on the breath;
come to rest in silence;
listening to
the sound of silence means
observing silence.

佛的體性是空；
佛的智慧是明；
佛的工作是慈悲。

Tranquility (śamatha) and insight (vipassanā)
Illuminating one's mind and recognizing
one's self-nature, cultivating seamless wisdom

The Buddha
has emptiness as his
essential nature;
light as his wisdom;
compassion as his activity.

Tranquility (śamatha) and insight (vipassanā)
Illuminating one's mind and recognizing
one's self-nature, cultivating seamless wisdom

Letting go is happiness;
compassion is good fortune.

心在覺性上，
光明無住，
心就能夠長久安住。

Tranquility (samatha) and insight (vipassanā)
Illuminating one's mind and recognizing
one's self-nature, cultivating seamless wisdom

止觀篇 智慧法語

The mind inclined to
enlightenment is
bright and flexible;
it's the mind of stability.

Tranquility (śamatha) and insight (vipassanā)
Illuminating one's mind and recognizing
one's self-nature, cultivating seamless wisdom

Use wisdom
to go beyond the world;
use loving kindness
to help and guide others.

行深般若波羅蜜多是
觀照的貫徹，
必須反覆地做，
才能貫徹此心。

Tranquility (śamatha) and insight (vipassanā)
Illuminating one's mind and recognizing
one's self-nature, cultivating seamless wisdom

止觀篇
智慧法語

Practicing
the perfection of wisdom
means thoroughly and
continuously observing
the mind.

什麼是自己？
所謂涅槃妙心、
實相無相、離一切相，
才是自己。

Tranquility (śamatha) and insight (vipassanā)
Illuminating one's mind and recognizing
one's self-nature, cultivating seamless wisdom

止觀篇 智慧法語

What is the self ?
It's the wonderful mind of
Nirvāna ,
the true form of no-form
that is beyond all forms.

「離相」才能成佛；
「離心意識」才能夠
自在。

Tranquility (śamatha) and insight (vipassanā)
Illuminating one's mind and recognizing
one's self-nature, cultivating seamless wisdom

Non-attachment to
appearances is a
prerequisite for
enlightenment;
the mind of
non-discrimination is a
prerequisite for
true freedom.

養成「禪修」的習慣，
就會慢慢帶出道心，
堅固道業。

Tranquility (śamatha) and insight (vipassanā)
Illuminating one's mind and recognizing
one's self-nature, cultivating seamless wisdom

As you get used to
meditation,
you gradually generate
the aspiration for
enlightenment and
become established
in the practice.

Tranquility (samatha) and insight (vipassanā)
Illuminating one's mind and recognizing
one's self-nature, cultivating seamless wisdom

All phenomena
are created by the mind;
how you look determines
what you see.

從「悲心」做起，
做到「明」、
做到「空」，
就會成佛。

Tranquility (śamatha) and insight (vipassanā)
Illuminating one's mind and recognizing
one's self-nature, cultivating seamless wisdom

止觀篇
智慧法語

Spiritual practice
begins with compassion,
proceeds to illumination and
emptiness, and culminates
in enlightenment.

永恆的生命叫「法身」；
無礙的智慧叫「報身」；
　大悲周遍叫「化身」。
從法、報、化三身學習，
　生命就會非常美好。

Tranquility (śamatha) and insight (vipassanā)
Illuminating one's mind and recognizing
one's self-nature, cultivating seamless wisdom

Eternal life is called
the "Dharma body";
unobstructed wisdom is called
the "enjoyment body";
all-pervading compassion is called
the "transformation body."
A life oriented towards
these three bodies of the Buddha
is a life imbued with happiness.

Tranquility (śamatha) and insight (vipassanā)
Illuminating one's mind and recognizing
one's self-nature, cultivating seamless wisdom

Sympathy is an innate
quality of human beings;
when confusion and
prejudice are put away,
compassion appears of
itself.

每個人都擁有覺性，
它是不死不滅的珍寶。

The nature of
enlightenment
is an innate quality;
it's an imperishable
treasure.

當心不起任何的煩惱，
就擁有了無礙的智慧。

When the mind doesn't
generate any defilements,
that's unobstructed wisdom.

Tranquility (śamatha) and insight (vipassanā)
Illuminating one's mind and recognizing
one's self-nature, cultivating seamless wisdom

Dedicating your practice to
Guanyin means cultivating
loving kindness and
compassion.
Loving kindness means
causing happiness,
compassion means
eliminating suffering.

欲望的止息需要智慧，
而無窮的智慧
來自內在寧靜。

Tranquility (śamatha) and insight (vipassanā)
Illuminating one's mind and recognizing
one's self-nature, cultivating seamless wisdom

Bringing craving to an end
requires wisdom;
unlimited wisdom has
tranquility as its source.

在生活中常常
覺照自心，靈明不昧，
保有清楚、明白的心境。

Tranquility (samatha) and insight (vipassanā)
Illuminating one's mind and recognizing
one's self-nature, cultivating seamless wisdom

In the course of
everyday life,
maintain clarity of mind;
continually observe
your state of mind.

Tranquility (śamatha) and insight (vipassanā)
Illuminating one's mind and recognizing
one's self-nature, cultivating seamless wisdom

Comprehending
the nature of the mind,
abiding in illumination;
this is how to cultivate
the wisdom and
virtue of the Tathāgata.

Tranquility (śamatha) and insight (vipassanā)
Illuminating one's mind and recognizing
one's self-nature, cultivating seamless wisdom

What is
illumination of mind?
It's the absence of
confusion, delusion, and
attachment.

修行是
心行淨化的功夫，
不跟人計較，
不在乎好壞。

Tranquility (śamatha) and insight (vipassanā)
Illuminating one's mind and recognizing
one's self-nature, cultivating seamless wisdom

Spiritual practice is a
process of purification;
don't get caught up in
bickering and pettiness.

Tranquility (śamatha) and insight (vipassanā)
Illuminating one's mind and recognizing
one's self-nature, cultivating seamless wisdom

Chan means
cultivating the mind of
unobstructed wisdom;
it requires introspection and
inner awareness.

Taking suffering as
your teacher,
you are bound to succeed
in the practice;
realizing impermanence
takes you across
the sea of suffering.

以禪修為橋樑進入心，
讓我們的心屬於自己，
找回自己。

Tranquility (śamatha) and insight (vipassanā)
Illuminating one's mind and recognizing
one's self-nature, cultivating seamless wisdom

Use meditation practice
to find the mind,
enter into it, and
make it your own.

「眞心」就是空，
「妙用」就是非空、非有。

Tranquility (śamatha) and insight (vipassanā)
Illuminating one's mind and recognizing
one's self-nature, cultivating seamless wisdom

The "true mind" is
emptiness;
"marvelous function" is
neither abiding in emptiness
nor being.

我們的身體
如同一盞燈籠，
而「覺性」就像燈燭，
燈燭能夠照明一切，
沒有內、外之分。

The body is like a lamp with
enlightenment as its bulb;
the bulb of enlightenment
illuminates all things
so that there is no longer
a difference between
inside and outside.

Tranquility (śamatha) and insight (vipassanā)
Illuminating one's mind and recognizing
one's self-nature, cultivating seamless wisdom

For me, what people say is
not an obstruction;
it's like a green traffic light;
it doesn't generate
the red light of troubles.

Tranquility (śamatha) and insight (vipassanā)
Illuminating one's mind and recognizing
one's self-nature, cultivating seamless wisdom

Meditation is allowing
the mind to dwell in
its own place.

Tranquility (śamatha) and insight (vipassanā)
Illuminating one's mind and recognizing
one's self-nature, cultivating seamless wisdom

Bring the mind
to rest in the place beyond
attachment to the world.

Tranquility (śamatha) and insight (vipassanā)
Illuminating one's mind and recognizing
one's self-nature, cultivating seamless wisdom

Peaceful abiding in
your enlightened nature
generates energy;
in the midst of
arising and disappearing,
you can return to yourself.

As soon as you fully realize
the spirit of impermanence
and not-self, you enter into
the realm of liberation.

Tranquility (samatha) and insight (vipassanā)
Illuminating one's mind and recognizing
one's self-nature, cultivating seamless wisdom

The discriminating mind is
the source of saṃsāra;
if you enter practice guided
by the discriminating mind,
you end up just
quarreling with others.

Tranquility (śamatha) and insight (vipassanā)
Illuminating one's mind and recognizing
one's self-nature, cultivating seamless wisdom

Transform
greed into generosity,
hatred into compassion,
ignorance into listening to
the teachings and
reading scriptures.

學習放下
「執著」的想法，
一有掛慮
就立刻放下它，
這就是「自在」。

Learn to relax and
let go of attachment and
worry as soon as it arises.
This is freedom.

修行者
只有「無我」是舞台，
其他的舞台
都叫做輪迴生死。

For the spiritual aspirant,
"not-self" is the only
performance stage;
all other performance stages
keep you trapped in
saṃsāra.

Tranquility (samatha) and insight (vipassanā)
Illuminating one's mind and recognizing
one's self-nature, cultivating seamless wisdom

A tranquil mind
doesn't generate delusions.

找到自己便是永恆，
永恆就是我們的
本來面目。

Tranquility (samatha) and insight (vipassanā)
Illuminating one's mind and recognizing
one's self-nature, cultivating seamless wisdom

Get in touch with eternity;
eternity is your
original face.

心靈和各種知見交會時，
要做到念念清明，
並且放棄愚昧的想法。

When your views and
opinions come into play,
evaluate them
with a clear mind and
abandon whatever is
based on ignorance.

坐禪能夠
清淨意識的浮騰，
讓一切的外緣和
意識的種子都寂靜。

Tranquility (samatha) and insight (vipassanā)
Illuminating one's mind and recognizing
one's self-nature, cultivating seamless wisdom

Meditation calms down
the flighty mind;
it brings your conditioned
habits to rest.

Tranquility (śamatha) and insight (vipassanā)
Illuminating one's mind and recognizing
one's self-nature, cultivating seamless wisdom

Meditation brings
the mind back to zero;
return to yourself and then
set out afresh.

觀念就像是一座牢籠，
想法多，
牢籠也跟著變多，
產生更多的習氣。

Tranquility (śamatha) and insight (vipassanā)
Illuminating one's mind and recognizing
one's self-nature, cultivating seamless wisdom

Each and every view
is like a cage;
the more views you hold,
the more cages there are,
generating habitual
tendencies.

Tranquility (samatha) and insight (vipassanā)
Illuminating one's mind and recognizing
one's self-nature, cultivating seamless wisdom

Reading the scriptures
cleanses the mind,
meditation transforms
your habitual tendencies.

Tranquility (samatha) and insight (vipassanā)
Illuminating one's mind and recognizing
one's self-nature, cultivating seamless wisdom

Śamatha means
observing your mind,
not the constant changes of
the outside world.

心之道第三輯智慧法語

止觀篇-明心見性，生無漏智慧

心道法師語錄

總 策 劃：釋了意
主　　編：洪淑妍
責任編輯：林玉芬
英文翻譯：甘修慧
英文校對：Dr. Maria Reis Habito
美術設計：蒲思元
發 行 人：歐陽慕親
出版發行：財團法人靈鷲山般若文教基金會附設出版社
劃撥帳戶：財團法人靈鷲山般若文教基金會附設出版社
劃撥帳號：18887793
地址：23444新北市永和區保生路2號21樓
電話：(02)2232-1008
傳真：(02)2232-1010
網址：www.093books.com.tw
讀者信箱：books@ljm.org.tw
法律顧問：永然聯合法律事務所
印刷：大亞彩色印刷製版股份有限公司
初版一刷：2014年7月
定價：新台幣250元(1套4冊)
ISBN：978-986-6324-76-5
總 經 銷：飛鴻國際行銷股份有限公司

靈鷲山書網

版權所有，翻印必究

本書若有缺損，請寄回更換

The Way of Mind III : Words of wisdom Tranquility (śamatha) and insight (vipassanā) : Illuminating one's mind andrecognizing one's self nature, cultivating seamless wisdom

Words of Dharma Master Hsin Tao

General Planer: Ven.Liao Yi Shih

Editor in Chief: Hong, Shu-yan

Editor in Charge: Lin, Yu-fen

English Translator: Gan, Xiu-hui

English Proofreading: Dr. Maria Reis Habito

Art Editor: Pu, Szu-Yuan

Publisher: Ouyang, Mu-qin

Published by and The postal service is allocated: the Subsidiary Publishing House of the Ling Jiou Mountain Prajna Cultural Education Foundation

Account Number: 18887793

Address: 21F., No.2, Baosheng Rd., Yonghe Dist., New Taipei City 23444, Taiwan (R.O.C.)

Tel: (02)2232-1008

Fax: (02)2232-1010

Website: www.093books.com.tw

E-mail: books@ljm.org.tw

Legal Consultant: Y. R. Lee & Partners Attorneys at Law

Printing: Apex Printing Corporation

The First Printing of the First Edition: July 2014

List Price: NT$ 250 dollars(Four-Manual Set)

ISBN: 978-986-6324-76-5

Distributor : Flying Horn International Marketing Co., Ltd.

Copyright Reserved

Please return it for replacement if it has any defects.

國家圖書館出版品預行編目(CIP)資料

心之道智慧法語. 第三輯 / 洪淑妍主編.--初版.
-- 新北市 : 靈鷲山般若出版, 2014.07
　　冊 ； 公分
ISBN 978-986-6324-76-5(全套 : 精裝)

1. 佛教說法 2. 佛教教化法

225.4　　　　　　　　　　　103011796